dimensional
DELIGHTS

20 Folding Fabric Screens to Personalize, Embellish + Display

Liz Aneloski

C&T PUBLISHING

Text © 2005 Liz Aneloski

Artwork © 2005 C&T Publishing, Inc.

Publisher: Amy Marson

Editorial Director: Gailen Runge

Acquisitions Editor: Jan Grigsby

Editor: Lynn Koolish

Technical Editors: Gael Betts, Gayl Gallagher, Wendy Mathson

Copyeditor/Proofreader: Wordfirm, Inc.

Cover Designer: Kristy K. Zacharias

Design Director/Book Designer: Kristy K. Zacharias

Illustrator: Kiera Lofgreen

Production Assistant: Tim Manibusan

Photography: Luke Mulks

Published by C&T Publishing, Inc., P.O. Box 1456,
Lafayette, CA 94549

Library of Congress Cataloging-in-Publication Data

Aneloski, Liz,
    Dimensional delights : 20 folding fabric screens to personalize, embellish & display / Liz Aneloski.
      p. cm.
    Includes index.
      ISBN 1-57120-333-8 (paper trade)
  1. Screens. 2. Textile crafts. I. Title.
      TT899.45.A54 2005
      746—dc22
                    2005015386

Printed in Singapore

10 9 8 7 6 5 4 3 2 1

Dedication

To Mark, Amber, and Ashlyn—my loves, my inspiration

Acknowledgments

I would like to thank:

My friends and co-workers at C&T Publishing, for helping me stretch creatively using your wonderful ideas and suggestions

Dill Buttons, for your support and wonderful products

All the participants, whose work is pictured, for allowing me to use your images

Contents

Introduction

Get ready to have some fun. Making folding fabric screens is simple and fast, and it gives you the opportunity to make a gift for anyone on your list—or, of course, for yourself. You can freeze time by using photographs of special people in your life or choose the perfect theme.

The screens can be sewn, glued, or a combination of both. Think about what you like doing best—hand stitching, machine stitching, tying, or gluing—you'll have the most fun if you construct your screens using techniques you enjoy. And remember, even if I sewed embellishments onto a screen, you can glue them if you like.

Just keep in mind how the screen will be used. Do you want the embellishments attached permanently, or should they be temporary so they can be removed (maybe even used and played with) and then re-attached?

You can look at the pictures to see how the screens were designed and follow the guidelines for a particular screen, or you can design your own using the helpful instructions in the first few chapters. To get your creative juices flowing, look at the list of ideas in Choosing a Theme (pages 4–5).

Choosing

To get started, read the lists of ideas on these pages. If you have a particular person in mind or want to use a specific type of embellishment (buttons, letters, photographs), think about this as you read. By the time you're finished, I'm sure you'll find that you have enough ideas to last you a long time. Have fun and be creative.

Youth

- Little Cars
- Girl Thing
- Tea Party
- Baby
- Birth Announcements
- Princess
- Angel
- Knight
- Braces (on and off)
- Dolls
- Stuffed Animals
- Child's Firsts

Teen

- College
- Girlfriends
- Favorite Bands
- Clubs and Activities
- Movie Stars
- Awards and Achievements
- College Acceptance
- Fraternity/Sorority

Adult

- Library/Books
- New House
- Wine
- Parties

Sports

- Dance
- Hockey
- Soccer
- Tennis
- Fishing
- Golf
- Skiing
- Sports Teams
- Swimming
- Bowling
- Martial Arts

Family

- Parents
- Grandparents
- Children
- Family Reunion
- Family Tree
- Siblings
- Cousins
- Aunts/Uncles

Holidays

- Christmas
- Halloween
- Easter
- Fourth of July
- Valentine's Day
- St. Patrick's Day

a Theme

Celebrations

Wedding	Promotion
Graduation	Confirmation
Birth	New Job
Birthday	Engagement
Anniversary	Adoption
Baptism	

Miscellaneous

Sea Life	Fibers and Findings
Beach	Mountains
Penny Rug Style	Patriotic
Coffee	Tea

Pets

Dogs
Cats
Horses
Pot-Bellied Pigs
Fish
Birds

Seasons

Spring
Summer
Fall
Winter

Travel

Airplanes	RVing
Trains	Honeymoon
Vacations	Hiking
Cruise	Camping

Occupations

Military	Nurse
Pilot	Artist
Doctor	Computer Tech
Veterinarian	Editor
Dentist	Writer
Teacher	Hairdresser
Lawyer	Astronaut
Firefighter	Mechanic
Police Officer	
Realtor	

Hobbies

Gardening	Theater
Sewing	Card Games
Cooking	Board Games
Art	Fishing
Music	Tools

Gathering

This part is so much fun. We all like to collect things, and now you have a great reason to do just that. Think of gathering materials to embellish your screen as the chance to create a mini collection that reflects the person or subject you've chosen for your screen. If the screen will be within reach of, or played with by a small child, be sure the items you choose are child safe.

1. Inspiration

Sometimes an object is the inspiration for the theme. That's what happened for me with the *Readin' and Writin'* screen (pages 22–23). I saw the little horn-rim glasses while combing the aisles of a craft store and knew I had to do something to incorporate them with books.

If you want to make a screen for a particular person, but don't know exactly what to do, visit places that have items they love—a dance supply store for a niece who loves to dance; a hockey supply store for a nephew who's an avid player; a hardware store for a handy husband, father, brother, or daughter who loves to tinker; a park or garden supply store for a hiker or gardener.

Don't limit yourself to your first ideas. Keep an open mind and be creative. You never know what you might find that will be just the perfect item. Make your screens personal.

2. Finding Materials

Just look around—you can find materials in many places. Reproductions or facsimiles of items are often sold in craft and scrapbooking stores, but I prefer to use the real thing whenever possible. Try looking in the following places:

Craft store	Drug store
Fabric store	Baby supply store
Quilt shop	Department store
Dollhouse supply store	Garden supply store
Hardware store	Pet supply store
Sporting goods store	Around the house
Home improvement center	Personal collections
	Outdoors

In addition to your found theme materials, choose fabrics, papers, threads, fibers, ribbons, trims and braids, buttons, beads, letters—anything you can think of to incorporate with and enhance your found items.

Materials

3. Background Fabric

After you have gathered some materials and chosen some embellishments, choose a fabric for the screen background. Place the materials and embellishments on the fabric to be sure they show up. If you can't see your items, choose a fabric that is lighter or darker in color, or has a pattern that is not so busy.

4. Photographs

Photographs for dimensional screens can be printed on paper or fabric. They can be enlarged, reduced, or manipulated in a variety of ways, using a photocopy machine or any number of computer software or scanning options. (See Resources on page 63 for books on printing photos on fabric.)

Keep in Mind

Decide whether your screen will need to fold flat for storage or remain open and on display. If it must fold flat, use thin embellishments. If it can remain open, you have more options.

Attaching heavy items can create a bit of a challenge. Be sure they won't cause the screen to sag or fall over, and be sure you can attach them securely. Heavy items might need to be stitched on or glued with a heavy-duty glue (such as E6000), rather than glued with white tacky glue or hot glue.

Similar thinking is needed for fragile items. If you choose to use them, take precautions to prevent them from wrinkling or breaking—cover them with clear contact paper or glue or stitch securely. You also may want to give instructions to the recipient for proper care of his or her screen.

Decide whether the items will be permanent, or removable, like the cars on *2 Fast 4U* (pages 18–19) and the dolls on *Sleepytime Dolls* (pages 36–37).

Layout and

DETERMINING SCREEN SIZE AND SHAPE

If you want to design your own screens, here's what you need to know about planning and picking a screen size. Each screen is made of multiple panels. Use the following steps to work out the number, size, and shape of the panels that will express your chosen theme.

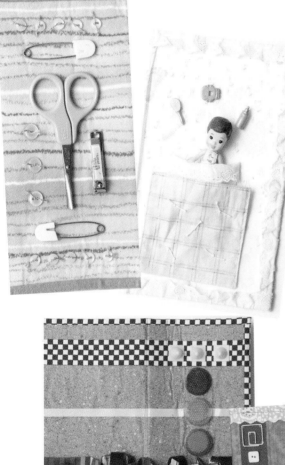

1. Lay Out Your Materials

After you have gathered the materials you want to use on your screen, or at least the materials you want to start with, lay them all out on your table.

2. Decide How to Attach Materials

Determine how you want to attach the embellishments. If you want them attached permanently, you will stitch or glue them to the screen. I stitch with perle cotton, quilting thread, or regular thread. For gluing, I use thick white tacky glue, hot glue, or heavy-duty E6000. Choose the method that makes the process the most enjoyable for you and that works the best for the use of the screen. For example, if a child will play with the screen, construct it to be as indestructible as possible.

3. Group the Items

Group some of the items you think might work especially well together to
see how they look. (A)

Think about how many panels you want your screen to have. Look
through the screens on pages 12–47 for ideas on the number and size of
screen panels. Your materials will help determine this. For example, if you
have four favorite groups of items, then maybe a four-panel screen would
be perfect. Arrange and rearrange the items into groups, one for each
panel, until you are happy with the layout. (B)

Fold your background fabric to the approximate size of the finished screen.
Place the items on the fabric. Place rulers along the top and side edges of
the fabric so you can start to get some idea of what sizes you want your
panels to be. (C)

A

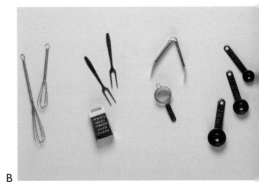

B

4. Determine the Panel Size

Divide the finished screen size into panels that will accommodate your
grouped embellishments. The panels can all be the same size, or they can
vary. If you will have similar items on each panel and want the spacing on
each panel to match, add ½″ extra to the outer edge of the side panels to
allow space for the edge finish. Again, look through the screens for ideas to
help guide you. If necessary, leave space for a title or other words. Add a
couple of extra inches to the total height of the screen—you'll trim the
panels to the exact size after attaching the embellishments.

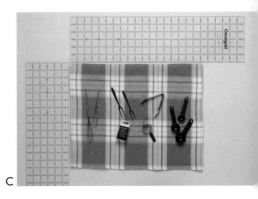

C

5. Record Your Measurements

Finalize the size of your screen panels and write the measurements on a
piece of paper. (D)

If you've chosen an unusual shape for the screen, draw the shape full-size
on paper.

Once you've determined the size and shape of your screen panels, you're
ready to construct your screen.

D

Constructing

Whether you're making a screen from this book or designing your own, now that you know the sizes and shapes of your screen panels, you're ready to construct your screen.

1. Gather Your Tools and Supplies

STIFF INTERFACING: I use fast2fuse Double-Sided Fusible Stiff Interfacing exclusively. It is ready to use, with fusible on both sides, and comes in regular weight for smaller, lighter projects, and heavyweight for larger or heavier projects. You may want to use two layers of regular weight if your screen needs more support. In place of fast2fuse, you may use very stiff interfacing and fusible web.

IRON: Any household iron is fine.

GLUES: Use hot glue when you need something to adhere immediately, E6000 for metal or heavy items, and thick white tacky glue for everything else. *Note:* Even if the items you are attaching are self-adhesive, it's best to use glue as well to make sure everything sticks to the fabric screen.

CUTTING TOOLS: A rotary cutter, ruler, and mat will give you the straightest cuts, but you can also use sharp scissors. You may want to use decorative rotary cutting blades or pinking shears for some screens.

FABRIC: Use fabric to cover the screens and for some edge-finishing treatments.

EMBELLISHMENTS: You can use ribbons, lace, tags, stick-on letters, metal clips, buttons—you name it.

EDGE FINISHES: In addition to fabric, you might use giant rickrack, rug binding, laces, and more. Check the materials list for the screen you are making or make up your own edge finish. See Finishing the Edges (pages 48–60).

THREAD: Choose regular cotton or polyester thread for machine sewing and heavier threads, such as perle cotton, for hand sewing.

NEEDLES: For hand sewing, use large-eye needles.

PAPER-BACKED FUSIBLE WEB: It's easier to fuse some of the flat decorations to the screens rather than glue them.

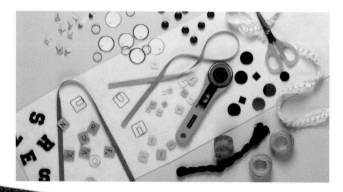

2. Prepare the Screen Panels

1. Cut the number, size, and shape of fast2fuse (or interfacing and fusible web) screen panels. Lay them out, leaving ⅛″ between the vertical edges (A). If you are using interfacing and fusible web, fuse the web to both sides of the interfacing.

2. Measure the total width of the screen panels and cut the fabric 2″–5″ wider than this measurement.

3. Measure the height of the screen panels and cut the fabric twice this measurement plus 4″. (B)

For example:

If there are 4 panels that are 4″ wide:

$$4″ \times 4 = 16″$$
$$\underline{+ \ 5″}$$
Cut the fabric 21″ wide

If the panels are 10″ high:

$$10″ \times 2 = 20″$$
$$\underline{+ \ 4″}$$
Cut the fabric 24″ high

4. Fold the fabric in half, top to bottom, with wrong sides together; press. (C)

3. Construct the Screen

1. With the fold of the fabric at the top edge, insert one of the screen panels between the layers of fabric. Align the top of the panel with the fold of the fabric and about 1″ from the raw side edge of the fabric. *Note:* If you are using Edge Finish #20 (see page 60), leave ¾″–1″ extra fabric at the folded edge. (D)

2. Fuse the first panel, making sure the panel doesn't shift.

3. Place the next screen panel between the layers of fabric as follows: Align the top edge as in Step 1, leaving ⅛″ space between this panel and the first panel. Fuse. Repeat for the remaining screen panels.

4. Turn the screen over (E). Fuse the fabric to the back of the screen.

5. Trim the excess fabric right next to the edges of the screen. *Note:* If you are using Edge Finish #20 (see page 60), leave ½″ of extra fabric on all 4 sides of the screen. (F)

6. Hand or machine stitch in the space between the screen panels to give them stability and to help the screen fold evenly. *For a no-sew option, omit this step.*

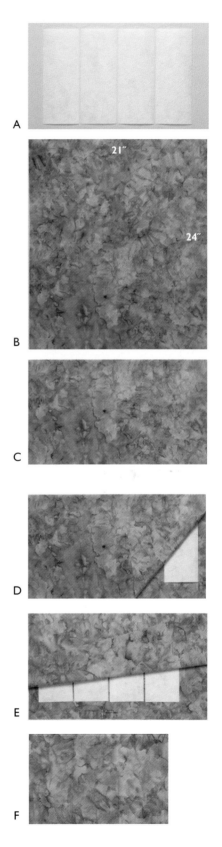

A

B

C

D

E

F

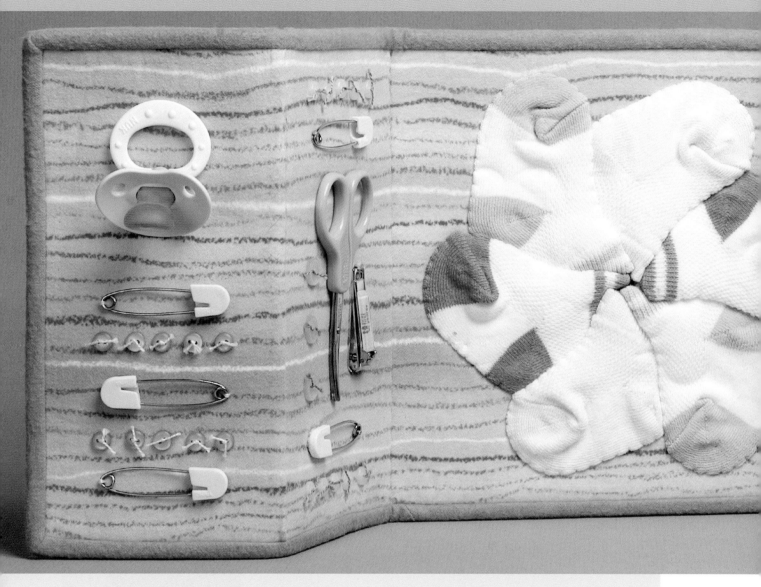

Baby Stuff

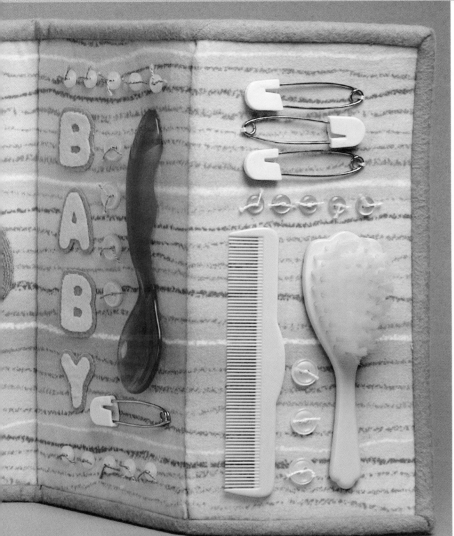

materials

See page 10 for basic supplies.

FLANNEL FABRICS: ¾ yard for screen,
¼ yard for edge finish
FAST2FUSE STIFF INTERFACING: ¼ yard
BABY ITEMS
BUTTONS: ½″ (10), ¼″ (35)
PERLE COTTON THREAD

screen panels

See page 11 for basic screen construction.

CENTER: 1 panel 8½″ × 8½″
INNER SIDES: 2 panels 4″ × 8½″
OUTER SIDES: 2 panels 4½″ × 8½″

edge finish

#1 (page 48)

- Add photos to personalize the screen.
- Use letters to spell out the baby's name.
- Attach baby items by sewing or gluing.

No-Sew

To make this screen completely no-sew, tie perle cotton
through the buttonholes, glue the buttons to the screen, and
choose one of the no-sew edge finishes (see pages 48–60).

Button Flowers

- Hand stitch perle cotton through the braided trim for the flower stems, then machine or hand stitch the cording to the screen.

- Use perle cotton thread to sew the leaf buttons to the screen.

- Tie the layered buttons together with ribbon, then attach them as one piece.

No-Sew

To make this screen completely no-sew, glue the cording to the screen for the stems, tie perle cotton through the buttonholes, and glue the buttons to the screen. Then choose one of the no-sew edge finishes (see pages 48–60).

materials

See page 10 for basic supplies.

COTTON FABRICS: ½ yard for screen, ¼ yard for edge finish

FAST2FUSE STIFF INTERFACING: ¼ yard

WOODEN BUTTONS: 1½″–1¼″ (24), ½″ (24), ½″–¾″ (10)

SQUARE BUTTONS: ⅜″–⅝″ (14)

RIBBON: ⅜″ wide (24 yards) for lattice, 1½″ wide (3 yards) for edge finish

RIBBON: ¼″ wide (1½ yards) to tie buttons

BRAIDED TRIM: ⅛″ wide (2 yards) for stems

PERLE COTTON THREAD: 2 yards

screen panels

See page 11 for basic screen construction.

4 panels 5″ × 6″

edge finish

#6 (page 50)

- Use perle cotton thread to sew a blanket stitch around the edges and to sew the buttons to the screen.
- Make cardboard or plastic templates to cut out the circle and square shapes.
- Choose from your button collection to feature your favorites.

No-Sew

To make this screen completely no-sew, omit the button-hole stitching, tie perle cotton through the buttonholes, and glue the buttons to the screen. Then choose one of the no-sew edge finishes (see pages 48–60).

materials

See page 10 for basic supplies.

WOOL FELT: ½ yard for screen, ¼ yard for edge finish

FAST2FUSE STIFF INTERFACING: ¼ yard

BUTTONS: 1⅝″ (5), ½″–¾″ (52)

PERLE COTTON THREAD

WOOL FELT SCRAPS for 3″ circles and 2″ squares

screen panels

See page 11 for basic screen construction.

CENTER: 3 panels 5″ × 6″

SIDES: 2 panels 5½″ × 6″

edge finish

#4 (page 50)

Buttons Galore

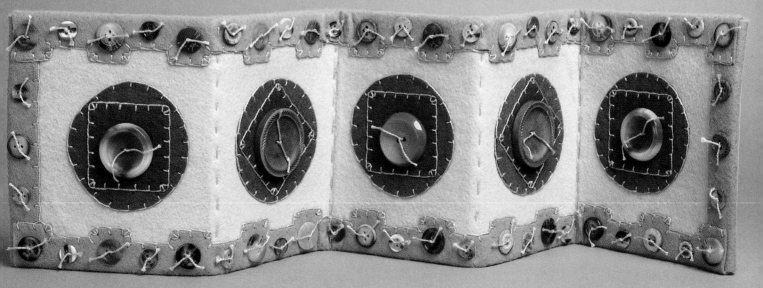

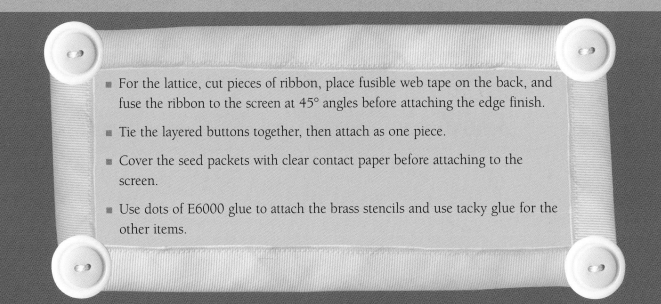

- For the lattice, cut pieces of ribbon, place fusible web tape on the back, and fuse the ribbon to the screen at 45° angles before attaching the edge finish.

- Tie the layered buttons together, then attach as one piece.

- Cover the seed packets with clear contact paper before attaching to the screen.

- Use dots of E6000 glue to attach the brass stencils and use tacky glue for the other items.

er Garden

materials

See page 10 for basic supplies and page 63 for resources.

COTTON FABRIC: $5/8$ yard for screen

FAST2FUSE STIFF INTERFACING: $1/4$ yard

RIBBON: $3/8''$ wide (24 yards) for lattice, $1 1/2''$ wide (3 yards) for edge finish

BRASS STENCILS: $2'' \times 6''$ (4), $2'' \times 3''$ (3)

FLOWER SEED PACKETS: 6

BRASS CLIPS: 18

BUTTONS: $5/8''$ white (24), $3/8''$ lavender (12), $3/8''$ green (12)

FUSIBLE WEB TAPE

CLEAR CONTACT PAPER (to cover and strengthen the seed packets)

PERLE COTTON THREAD

screen panels

See page 11 for basic screen construction.

CENTER: 1 panel $13 1/2'' \times 8 1/2''$

INNER SIDES: 2 panels $6 3/4'' \times 8 1/2''$

OUTER SIDES: 2 panels $6 1/2'' \times 8 1/2''$

edge finish

#16 (page 58)

No-Sew

To make this screen completely no-sew, choose one of the no-sew edge finishes (see pages 48–60).

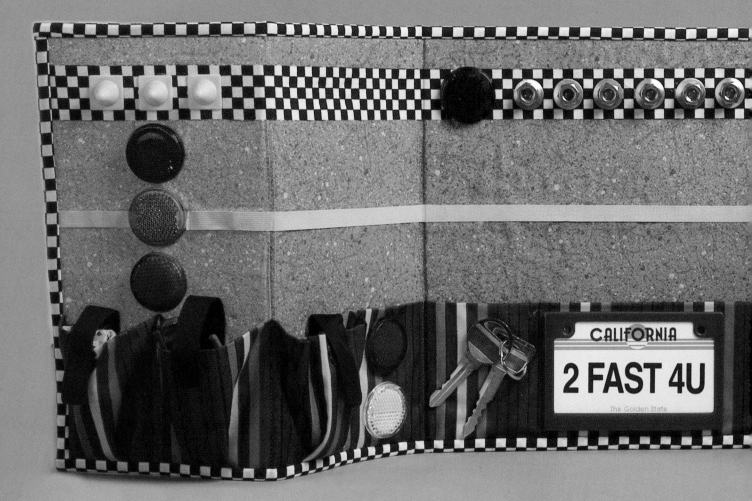

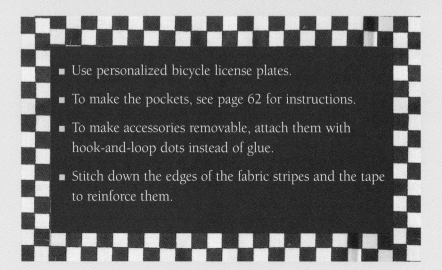

- Use personalized bicycle license plates.

- To make the pockets, see page 62 for instructions.

- To make accessories removable, attach them with hook-and-loop dots instead of glue.

- Stitch down the edges of the fabric stripes and the tape to reinforce them.

2 Fast 4U

materials

See page 10 for basic supplies.

COTTON FABRICS: ¾ yard for screen, ¼ yard for edge finish and stripe

FAST2FUSE STIFF INTERFACING: ⅜ yard

TOY VEHICLES

VEHICLE ACCESSORIES

NUTS AND WASHERS

CLOTH TAPE (cut to ½″)

HOOK-AND-LOOP STRAPS AND DOTS

PAPER-BACKED FUSIBLE WEB for checked stripe

screen panels

See page 11 for basic screen construction.

CENTER: 1 panel 10″ × 10″

SIDES: 4 panels 5″ × 10″

edge finish

#2 (page 49)

No-Sew

To make this screen completely no-sew, choose one of the no-sew edge finishes (see pages 48–60). Keep in mind that if the screen will be played with, sewing the edges and the pockets will make the screen hold up better.

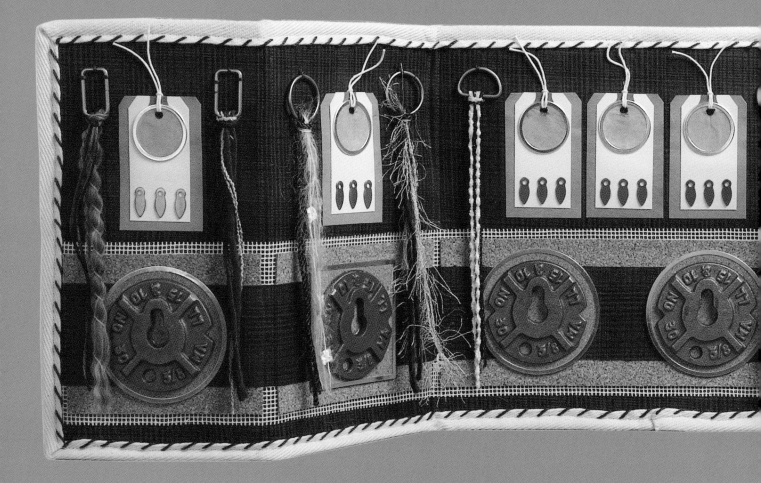

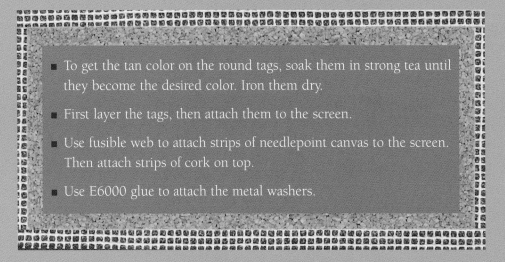

- To get the tan color on the round tags, soak them in strong tea until they become the desired color. Iron them dry.

- First layer the tags, then attach them to the screen.

- Use fusible web to attach strips of needlepoint canvas to the screen. Then attach strips of cork on top.

- Use E6000 glue to attach the metal washers.

materials

See page 10 for basic supplies.

COTTON FABRIC: ¾ yard for screen and strip

RUG BINDING: 3 yards for edge finish

FAST2FUSE STIFF INTERFACING: ¾ yard

MALLEABLE WASHERS: 2½″ (6) (ask for them at a hardware store)

TAGS: 1⅜″ × 2¾″ white (7), 2″ × 3″ brown (7)

METAL TABS: 21

NEEDLEPOINT CANVAS FOR TRIM

SHEET CORK

CORK TAGS: 3″ squares and circles

YARNS: assorted types and colors

METAL RINGS: assorted sizes and shapes (10)

PERLE COTTON THREAD

PAPER-BACKED FUSIBLE WEB

screen panels

See page 11 for basic screen construction.

CENTER: 1 panel 10″ × 10″

SIDES: 4 panels 5″ × 10″

edge finish

#7 (page 51)

No-Sew

To make this screen completely no-sew, tie yarn to the rings before gluing them to the screen. Then choose one of the no-sew edge finishes (see pages 48–60).

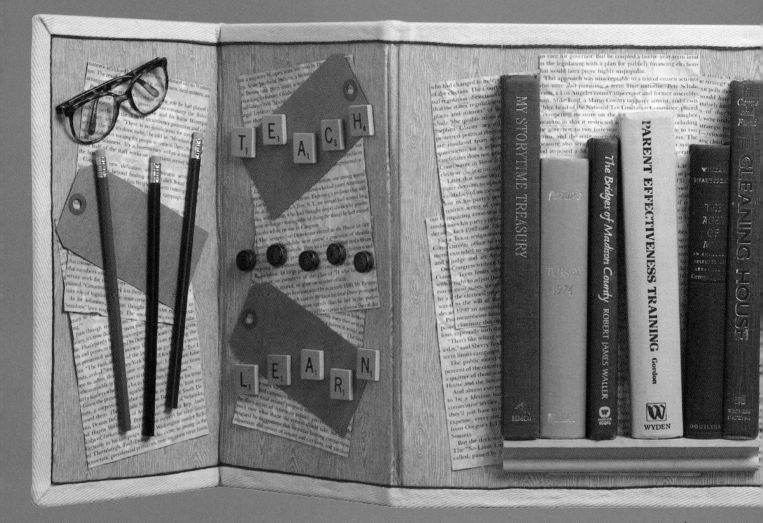

- Cut the book pages to size, scrunch each page into a tight ball, open out flat, soak in strong tea until it becomes the desired color, and iron dry and flat.

- Use an electric saw to cut the book binding sections to varying thicknesses.

- For a classic look, choose fabric- or leather-bound books.

- Wood-grain fabric makes a great screen background.

and Writin'

materials

See page 10 for basic supplies.

COTTON FABRIC: ¾ yard for screen

RUG BINDING: 3 yards for edge finish

FAST2FUSE STIFF INTERFACING: ¾ yard

HARDCOVER BOOKS

TEA-DYED BOOK PAGES

SCRABBLE BOARD GAME LETTER HOLDER

TAGS: 2½″ × 4¾″ (6)

PENCILS: 6

GLASSES: 2 pairs

LETTERS: Scrabble letter tiles and typewriter keys

PERLE COTTON THREAD

screen panels

See page 11 for basic screen construction.

CENTER: 1 panel 12″ × 12″

SIDES: 4 panels 6″ × 12″

edge finish

#10 (page 54)

hockey

score

Z-CAR

NO7

TRENT

- Cut pieces of string and place them at 45° angles across the center panel. Hot glue the ends on the center panel, just inside where the screen will fold. Glue the hockey stick pieces over the ends of the string, making sure the screen will still fold.

- Cut foam sheets for photo frames.

- Personalize the screen by using your player's name and team name.

- Fuse fabric to the screen for face-off circles and goalie cages.

materials

See page 10 for basic supplies and page 63 for resources.

COTTON FABRICS: ¾ yard for screen, scraps for rink markings and goals

HOCKEY SKATE LACES: 96″ (2) for edge finish

FAST2FUSE STIFF INTERFACING: ¾ yard

PHOTOGRAPHS: 4¼″ round (2), 3½″ round (2), 5″ × 7″ (1)

CLOTH TAPE for rink stripes (cut to ⅛″ and ¼″)

FOAM RUBBER SHEET for photo frames

FOAM RUBBER STARS

FOAM RUBBER LETTERS

WOODEN HOCKEY STICK PIECES

NYLON CORD

PAPER-BACKED FUSIBLE WEB

screen panels

See page 11 for basic screen construction.

CENTER: 1 panel 10½″ × 11½″

SIDES: 2 panels 10″ × 11½″

edge finish

#8 (page 52)

For other sports, think about what "says" that sport: For baseball, instead of hockey sticks, find a toy bat that can be cut in half. For basketball, use a hoop and net; for football, the goalposts.

Pinwheel Frames

- Pick a screen fabric that emphasizes your chosen theme.

- Cut the burlap 1″ larger than the grouped photo frames, embellish with stitching, then fuse to the screen.

- Be sure to find four horizontal photos and four vertical photos.

- If the photo frames are magnetic, remove the magnets before gluing them to the screen.

No-Sew

To make this screen completely no-sew, replace the decorative stitching with glued-on embellishments. Then choose one of the no-sew edge finishes (see pages 48–60).

materials

See page 10 for basic supplies.

COTTON FABRIC: ¾ yard for screen

FAST2FUSE STIFF INTERFACING: ⅜ yard

BURLAP: ¼ yard for frame background, ¼ yard for edge finishing

PHOTOGRAPHS: 2¼″ x 3½″ (8)

PLEXIGLAS FRAMES: 2¼″ x 3½″ (8)

PERLE COTTON THREAD

PAPER-BACKED FUSIBLE WEB

screen panels

See page 11 for basic screen construction.

2 panels 10″ x 10″

edge finish

#9 (see page 53)

- Remove the flowers from the stems and trim off any excess stem before attaching.

- Glue the ribbon onto the photograph and invitation first, so you can fold the ends of the ribbon to the back for a clean edge.

- Use doilies under the photograph and invitation.

- Use an edge trim that's similar to the doilies for a cohesive look.

materials

See page 10 for basic supplies.

COTTON FABRIC: ¾ yard for screen
FAST2FUSE STIFF INTERFACING: ¼ yard
TRIM: 1½ yards for edge finishing
RIBBON: 1″ wide (1½ yards) for edge finishing, ⅜″ wide (1½ yards) for photo frames
PHOTOGRAPH: 5″ x 7″
INVITATION
DOILIES: larger than the photo and invitation
SILK FLOWERS

screen panels

See page 11 for basic screen construction.

2 panels 8½″ x 12″

edge finish

#17 (see page 58)

1930 Wedding

G

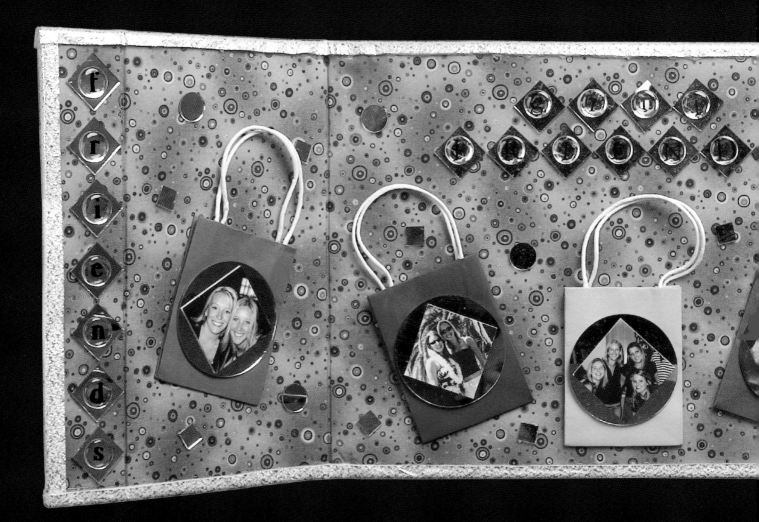

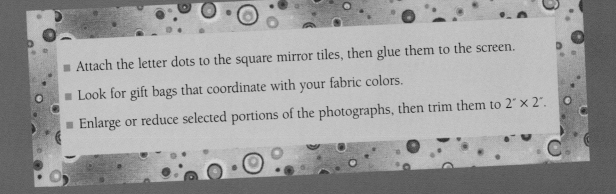

■ Attach the letter dots to the square mirror tiles, then glue them to the screen.

■ Look for gift bags that coordinate with your fabric colors.

■ Enlarge or reduce selected portions of the photographs, then trim them to 2″ × 2″.

materials

See page 10 for basic supplies and page 63 for resources.

COTTON FABRIC: ¾ yard for screen

METALLIC SILVER POLAR FLEECE: ¼ yard for edge finish

FAST2FUSE STIFF INTERFACING: ¾ yard

PHOTOGRAPHS: 2″ × 2″ (5)

SMALL GIFT BAGS: 4″ × 5″ (5)

MIRROR TILES: 3″ circles (5), 1″ squares (25), ¾″ circles (7), ½″ squares (11)

SELF-ADHESIVE LETTER DOTS

screen panels

See page 11 for basic screen construction.

CENTER: 1 panel 16″ × 11½″

INNER SIDES: 2 panels 10″ × 11½″

OUTER SIDES: 2 panels 2″ × 11½″

edge finish

#5 (page 50)

- Fuse fabric strips to the inner side panels.

- Frame the tags with fabric cut $\frac{1}{8}''$ larger all around. Fuse the fabric to the screen.

- Tie perle cotton thread to the round tags before attaching them to the screen.

- Keep the clear plastic makeup covers and glue them to the open cases.

- For added stability, back the screen with mat board.

Girl Thing

materials

See page 10 for basic supplies and page 63 for resources.

COTTON FABRICS: ¾ yard for screen, ¼ yard for edge finish, scraps for inner side panels and to frame tags

FAST2FUSE STIFF INTERFACING: ¾ yard

GIRL STUFF

METAL CLIPS: 22

PREPRINTED PHRASES on clear backgrounds

SELF-ADHESIVE WORD DOTS

TAGS: 2″ × 4″ (2), 1¼″ circles (13)

GIFT BAG: 4½″ × 5½″

BUTTONS: ⅜″–½″ (8)

PERLE COTTON THREAD

PAPER-BACKED FUSIBLE WEB

screen panels

See page 11 for basic screen construction.

CENTER: 1 panel 14″ × 10″

INNER SIDES: 2 panels 1½″ × 10″

OUTER SIDES: 2 panels 7″ × 10″

edge finish

#3 (page 50)

No-Sew

To make this screen completely no-sew, choose one of the no-sew edge finishes (see pages 48–60).

- Trim the undulating edge after constructing the screen but before adding embellishments.

- Tear the sandpaper strips for a more natural, random edge; experiment to get the look you want.

- A circle cutter will make perfect circles. Or, use sharp scissors and a circle template.

in the Sun

fun

materials

See page 10 for basic supplies and page 63 for resources.

COTTON FABRIC: $\frac{7}{8}$ yard for screen

GIANT JUMBO RICKRACK: 3 yards for edge finish

FAST2FUSE STIFF INTERFACING: $\frac{3}{8}$ yard

FLIP-FLOPS: women's size 5 (3 pairs)

SUNGLASSES: 2 pairs

SELF-ADHESIVE LETTER DOTS

PHOTOGRAPHS: $3\frac{3}{4}''$ circles (6)

SANDPAPER: 2 grits with different textures

SEASHELLS

FOAM RUBBER LETTERS

CARD STOCK for photo frames and title circles

screen panels

See page 11 for basic screen construction.

CENTER: 1 panel $10'' \times 13''$

SIDES: 2 panels $10\frac{1}{2}'' \times 13''$

edge finish

#11 (page 55)

- Cut the screen panels. Mark and trim the curved edge, then construct the screen.
- Draw the letters or use a computer font to create letters about 3½″ tall. Trace them onto the paper side of the fusible web (remember to reverse the letters when you trace them). Fuse the letters and stars to the fabric, cut them out, and then fuse the cut-out letters to the screen.

America

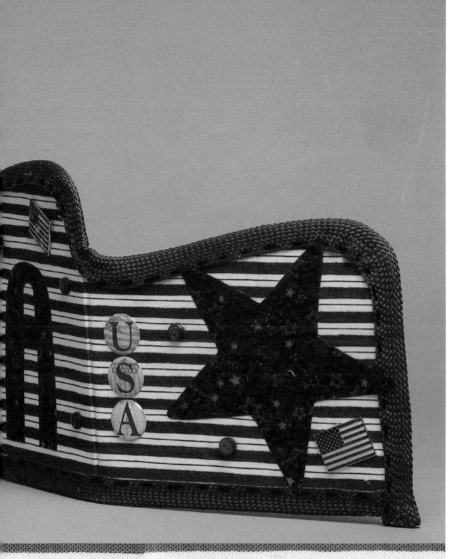

materials

See page 10 for basic supplies and page 63 for resources.

COTTON FABRICS: ⅝ yard for screen, scraps for letters and stars

PREFOLDED TRIM: 3 yards for edge finish

FAST2FUSE STIFF INTERFACING: ½ yard

SELF-ADHESIVE LETTER DOTS

PREPRINTED PATRIOTIC WORDS AND STARS

BUTTONS: ¼″ (15)

FLAG TACK PINS: 5

PERLE COTTON THREAD

PAPER-BACKED FUSIBLE WEB

screen panels

See page 11 for basic screen construction and page 60 for star and curve patterns.

PANEL 1: 6″ × 9″

PANEL 2: 6″ × 8″

PANEL 3: 6″ × 7″

PANEL 4: 6″ × 6″

PANEL 5: 6″ × 5″

edge finish

#19 (page 59)

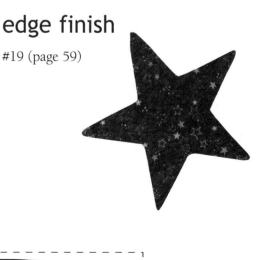

No-Sew

To make this screen completely no-sew, choose one of the no-sew edge finishes (see pages 48–60).

Top edge of panel fabric

Cut on solid line

Cutting Guide

- See page 61 for instructions on making the pockets and quilts.

- Use a hook-and-loop dot on each pocket and quilt.

- Stagger the placement of the doll beds to make folding the screen easier.

time Dolls

materials

See page 10 for basic supplies.

COTTON FABRICS: ⅝ yard for screen, ¼ yard or scraps for quilts

EYELET FABRIC: ⅛ yard for doll pockets

EYELET TRIM: 2½ yards

FAST2FUSE STIFF INTERFACING: ½ yard

DOLLS: 1″ × 3″ (5)

DOLL ACCESSORIES

PERLE COTTON THREAD

HOOK-AND-LOOP DOTS: 5

screen panels

See page 11 for basic screen construction.

CENTER: 3 panels 5″ × 9½″

SIDES: 2 panels 5½″ × 9½″

edge finish

#13 (page 56)

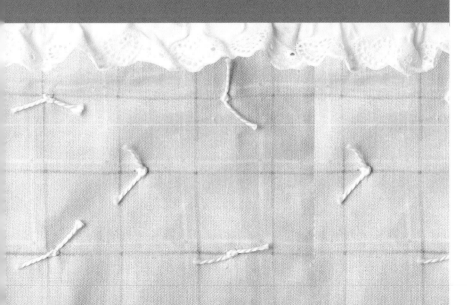

Divas

- Paint the tins with acrylic paint. Allow them to dry, then sponge gold paint over the color.
- Use a computer to print the words on an 8½" × 11" piece of brown kraft paper, or use press-on letters. Trim to size and glue to the layered tags.

on Parade

materials

See page 10 for basic supplies and page 63 for resources.

COTTON FABRIC: ¾ yard for screen and inside of tins

NONSKID CONTACT PAPER or drawer liner for edge finish

FAST2FUSE STIFF INTERFACING: ¾ yard

SCRABBLE LETTER TILES for legs and arms (40)

BUTTONS:

For the heads: 1″ wooden for face (5), ⅜″ for the eyes (10), ⅛″ black for the eyes (10)

For the legs and arms: ⅝″ (20), ½″ (20)

For the hands and feet: ½″ wooden (20), ⅜″ colored (20)

WOOD CIRCLES: 1½″ for the heads (5)

SEED BEADS to cover the buttonholes: 120

SMALL GIFT BAGS: 3¼″ × 4¼″ (5)

TAGS: 2″ × 2¾″ (5)

SMALL MINT TINS: 2″ × 2½″ (5)

ACRYLIC PAINT

HEART CHARMS: large (5), small gold (5)

BROWN KRAFT PAPER for layered tags and labels

GROSGRAIN RIBBON: ⅜″ (2 yards) for arms and legs

screen panels

See page 11 for basic screen construction.

CENTER: 3 panels 6″ × 12″

SIDES: 2 panels 7″ × 12″

edge finish

#14 (page 57)

■ Trim cotton fabric to size and cover the inside of the tins. Place a large painted heart inside each tin.

■ To make the arms and legs: Layer the buttons and beads on the tiles. Glue lengths of grosgrain ribbon to the tin, glue on the layered tiles, and trim the excess ribbon.

- Use words that characterize your pet.

- Enlarge a photograph of your pet's head to use as a pattern for the background silhouette.

- Trace the silhouette on the paper side of the fusible web (remember to reverse the image when tracing). Fuse the silhouette to fabric, cut out, and fuse to the screen.

avorite Pet

materials

See page 10 for basic supplies and page 63 for resources.

COTTON FABRICS: ¾ yard for screen, scraps for silhouettes

RIBBON: 1½" wide (5¼ yards) for edge finish

NARROW DOG LEASH: approximately ⅜" × 94" for edge finish

FAST2FUSE STIFF INTERFACING: ¾ yard

PHOTOGRAPHS: 3"–3½" circles (3), 2" x 2" (6)

FELT PHOTO FRAMES

FOAM RUBBER LETTERS

SLIDE MOUNTS: 2" × 2" (6)

SMALL DOG COLLARS: 3

SMALL RAWHIDE BONES: 2

PAPER-BACKED FUSIBLE WEB

screen panels

See page 11 for basic screen construction.

CENTER: 1 panel 10" × 11"

SIDES: 2 panels 10½" × 11"

edge finish

#12 (page 55)

■ Another option is to use paper for the silhouettes, which can be glued to the screens.

■ Enlarge or reduce selected portions of the photographs, then trim to 3" or 3½" circles. A circle cutter will make perfect circles. Or, use sharp scissors and a circle template.

- Use sheer ribbon on the edges of the photographs and slide mounts. Glue the ribbon on the edges of the slide mounts to form frames.

- Enlarge or reduce selected portions of the photographs, then trim to fit the slide mounts.

- Use both satin and grosgrain ribbons on the edge treatment for an interesting texture.

Dance

materials

See page 10 for basic supplies and page 63 for resources.

COTTON FABRIC: ¾ yard for screen

RIBBON: ½″ wide (3 yards) for edge finish, 1″ wide (3 yards) for edge finish, ⅜″ wide (4 yards) for photo frames

FAST2FUSE STIFF INTERFACING: ¾ yard

PHOTOGRAPHS: 1½″ × 1½″ to 5″ × 7″

SLIDE MOUNTS: 3½″ × 3½″ (2), 2″ × 2″ (2)

SELF-ADHESIVE LETTER DOTS

MIRROR TILES: 1″ round (5), 1″ square (17), ¾″ round (12)

screen panels

See page 11 for basic screen construction.

CENTER: 1 panel 10″ × 10½″

SIDES: 2 panels 10½″ × 10½″

edge finish

#18 (page 58)

This is a great format to feature any activity—drama, music, sports—or just to display a group of photos.

's Cookin'?

materials

See page 10 for basic supplies and page 63 for resources.

KITCHEN TOWEL: at least 18″ × 25″ for screen

BROWN KRAFT PAPER for edge finish

CLEAR PACKAGING TAPE for edge finish

FAST2FUSE STIFF INTERFACING: ½ yard

SMALL KITCHEN UTENSILS

SMALL RECIPE CARDS

CARD STOCK for title letters

screen panels

See page 11 for basic screen construction.

CENTER: 2 panels 4″ × 12″

SIDES: 2 panels 4½″ × 12″

edge finish

#15 (page 57)

- Choose a kitchen towel that matches your kitchen décor.

- Make reduced color photocopies of your favorite recipe cards.

- Print computer-generated lettering (about 1″ high) on card stock for the title or use press-on letters.

- Layer the title card stock before gluing it to the screen.

GONE FISHING

to Collage

materials

See page 10 for basic supplies.
COTTON FABRIC: ¾ yard for screen
FAST2FUSE STIFF INTERFACING: ½ yard
PHOTOGRAPHS
FISHING LURES
CARD STOCK

screen panels

See page 11 for basic screen construction.
CENTER: 1 panel 6½″ × 14″
SIDES: 2 panels 7″ × 14″

edge finish

#20 (page 60)

- Enlarge or reduce selected portions of the photographs, then trim them to size. I cut photos to 1⅞″ squares to fill in the spaces, then I trimmed the larger snapshots to fit.

- Print computer-generated lettering on card stock for the title or use press-on letters.

- Use wire cutters to cut off the sharp tips of the hooks on the lures.

This is a great format to feature any group of photos. Find a screen fabric that goes with your chosen theme, and then add a few three-dimensional mementos.

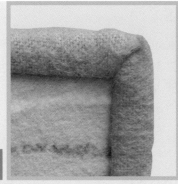

#1

pages 12-13

French Double-Fold With Mitered Corners

1. Measure around the screen, then add 12″ to this measurement.

2. Cut enough 2¼″-wide binding strips to total the measurement from Step 1. Stitch the strips into a long strip, using diagonal seams.

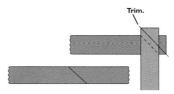

Trim.

3. Turn under the beginning end ¼″ and press. Fold the binding strips in half lengthwise and press.

4. Match the raw edges of the binding strip to the front of the bottom edge of the screen. Start stitching 4″ from the end of the binding strip (using a ¼″ seam allowance) and stop stitching ¼″ from the corner. Backtack, lift the presser foot, and cut the threads.

5. Rotate the screen 90° and fold the binding straight up so the fold forms a 45° angle.

6. Fold the binding straight down, matching the raw edge to the edge of

the screen. Beginning with a back-tack, stitch the next side.

7. Repeat for all sides. Stop stitching about 1″ from the beginning end of the binding and backtack. Overlap this end of the binding with the starting end of the binding and trim, leaving a 1″ tail to tuck into the fold of the starting end.

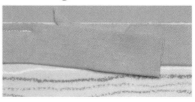

8. Tuck the end of the binding into the fold of the starting end, pin in place, and stitch.

9. Fold the binding over the edge to the back of the screen, pin, and hand stitch.

I prefer to finish the edges before adding the embellishments. It's easier to maneuver the screen while it's flat and lightweight.

French Double-Fold With Butted Corners

pages 18-19

1. Measure the sides of the screen, then add 2″ to this measurement.

2. Use the measurement from Step 1 to cut 2 binding strips 2¼″ wide.

3. Fold the binding strips in half lengthwise and press.

4. Match the raw edges of a binding strip to the front of a side edge of the screen, allowing the binding to extend 1″ past the corners on both ends. Stitch from end to end, using a ¼″ seam allowance.

5. Trim the excess strip fabric even with the edges of the screen.

6. Repeat for the other side of the screen. Fold the binding over the edge to the back of the screen and hand stitch.

7. Measure the top and bottom edges, then add 3″ to this measurement.

8. Use the measurement from Step 7 to cut 2 binding strips 2¼″ wide.

9. Fold the binding in half lengthwise and press.

10. Match the raw edges of a binding strip to the bottom edge of the screen, allowing the binding to extend 1½″ past the corners on both ends.

11. Stitch from end to end, using a ¼″ seam allowance. Trim the end of the binding, leaving ½″ extending past the corner of the screen.

12. Repeat for the top edge of the screen.

13. Fold the binding up and fold the ends to the back of the screen.

14. Fold the binding over the edge to the back of the screen, pin, and hand stitch.

Raw Edge With Butted Corners

1. Measure the sides of the screen, then add 2″ to this measurement.

2. Use the measurement from Step 1 to cut 2 binding strips 1½″ wide. Cut with a straight or decorative edge or use a rotary cutter with a decorative-edge blade.

3. Measure the top and bottom edges, then add 3″ to this measurement.

4. Use the measurement from Step 3 to cut 2 binding strips 1½″ wide, as in Step 2. For Edge Finish #4, cut the strips 2″ wide.

5. Fold the strips in half lengthwise and press. For Edge Finish #4: Open both strips, make ½″ cuts every 1″, and trim along the edge to the shape shown.

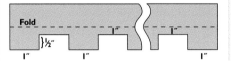

6. Place one of the shorter strips over the front of a side edge of the screen, lining up the fold on the strip with the edge of the screen. Trim the end of the strip even with the edge of the screen.

7. Either machine stitch, hand button hole stitch, or glue to attach the strip to the side edge of the screen. If buttonhole stitching or gluing, repeat to attach the strip to the back of the screen.

8. Repeat for the other side edge and then for the top and bottom edges of the screen.

Rug Binding With Mitered Corners

1. Measure around the perimeter of the screen, then add 12″ to this measurement.

2. Use the measurement from Step 1 to cut a piece of rug binding. Cut a piece of perle cotton thread twice as long as the cut rug binding.

3. Place a pin in the center of a long edge of the rug binding.

4. Thread a needle with the perle cotton. Insert the needle into the binding at the pin, ¼″ from the edge, and pull half the length of the thread through the binding.

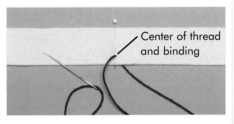

Center of thread and binding

5. Use a whip stitch to stitch to one end of the binding. Remove the needle from the thread, leaving the thread tail.

6. Rethread the needle with the other end of the thread and rotate the binding 180°.

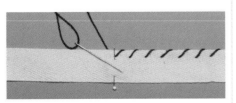

7. Use a whip stitch to stitch to the other end. Remove the needle, leaving the thread tail.

8. Fold the binding in half lengthwise and press.

9. Match the fold in the binding with the edge of the screen. Start stitching 2″ from the end of the binding, stopping 1″ from the first corner.

10. Wrap the binding around the corner. Be sure the fold of the binding is aligned with the edge of the screen.

11. Fold the binding, on the top and underneath, into a miter.

12. Stitch to the exact edge of the miter fold. With the needle down, pivot to turn the corner.

pages 20-21

#7

13. Repeat around the entire edge, stopping 2″ from where you started. Trim the binding, leaving a 1″ overlap of the ends.

14. Fold under the raw end of the binding ¼″. Position the second end on top of the first end and finish stitching.

#8

pages 24-25

Skate Laces With Rounded Corners

1. Mark the corners of the screen with a curve using a compass, a circle template, a small glass, or anything that is the correct size. Trim.

2. Measure around the screen, then add 12″. Purchase skate laces a minimum of this length.

3. On the front of the screen, mark the middle of the bottom edge with a pin. On the top edge of the screen, mark the middle of the screen with a pin, then place a pin ½″ from each side of the center pin.

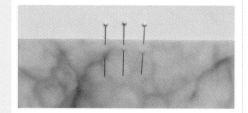

4. Remove the center pin.

5. Place the center of one of the laces on the bottom-edge pin, with half the width of the lace on the screen and half off the edge.

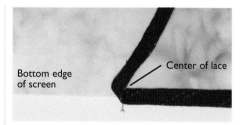

Bottom edge of screen — Center of lace

6. Hot glue the lace to the screen, starting at the pin and ending at the first top-edge pin you come to.

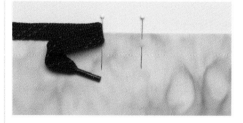

7. Repeat for the other half of the lace. Remove the pins and tie the ends of the lace in a knot.

8. Turn the screen to the back and repeat the process, aligning the second lace behind the first but this time gluing the second lace to both the screen *and* the first lace.

Single-Fold With Butted Corners

page 26

1. Measure the sides of the screen, then add 2″ to this measurement.

2. Use the measurement from Step 1 to cut 2 binding strips 1½″ wide.

3. Working in short sections on the front of the screen, place a line of hot glue ⅛″ from the edge of the screen. Then match the raw edge of a binding strip to a side edge of the screen, allowing the binding to extend past the corner of the screen.

4. Trim the excess strip fabric even with the edges of the screen. Repeat for the other side of the screen.

5. Fold the binding over the edge to the back of the screen. Turn under the raw edge of the binding ¼″.

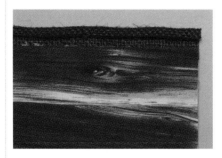

6. Hot glue the binding to the back of the screen.

7. Measure the top and bottom edges, then add 3″ to this measurement.

8. Use the measurement from Step 7 to cut 2 binding strips 1½″ wide.

9. Match the raw edge of a binding strip to the bottom edge of the screen, allowing the binding to extend past the corner of the screen.

Trim the excess binding, leaving ½″ to extend past the edge of the screen.

10. Fold the excess binding to the front and hot glue in place.

11. Fold the long edge of the binding to the back of the screen, fold under ¼″, and hot glue as you did for the side binding.

#10

pages 22-23

Rug Binding With Mitered Corners

1. Measure around the perimeter of the screen, then add 12″ to this measurement.

2. Use the measurement from Step 1 to cut a piece of rug binding.

3. Fold the binding in half lengthwise and press.

4. Working in short sections on the front of the bottom edge of the screen, place a line of hot glue ¼″ from the edge of the screen. Place binding matching the fold on the binding with the edge of the screen.

5. Stop gluing ½″ from the corner. Start gluing ½″ from the corner on the next side of the screen.

6. Wrap the binding around the corner and place it on the hot glue. Be sure the fold of the binding is aligned with the edge of the screen.

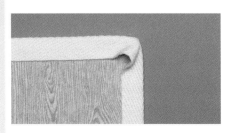

7. Go back and fold the binding into a miter and secure with hot glue.

8. Repeat around the entire edge, stopping 2″ from where you started. Trim the binding, leaving a 1″ overlap of the ends.

9. Fold under the raw end of the binding ¼″ and secure with hot glue.

10. Hot glue the remaining section. Repeat to attach the binding to the back of the screen.

11. Starting and finishing in one corner, refer to the project photo to hot glue perle cotton thread along the edge of the binding, using the tiniest line of hot glue possible.

Rounded Corners

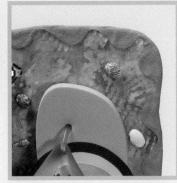

#11

Rickrack/Ribbon
pages 32-33

#12

Layered Trim/Ribbon
pages 40-41

1. Mark the corners with a curve. For #11: Use a rotary cutter to trim or freehand cut an undulating edge around the edge of the screen. Be sure to leave some of the original edge on each edge of the screen so it will maintain its original rectangular shape and will stand straight.

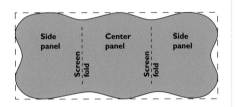

2. Measure around the screen, then add 8″ to this measurement.

3. Use the measurement from Step 2 to cut a piece of rickrack or ribbon.

4. Fold the rickrack or ribbon in half lengthwise and press.

5. Starting on the bottom edge and working in short sections on the front of the screen, place a line of hot glue right next to the edge of the rickrack or ribbon. Match the fold on the rickrack or ribbon with the edge of the screen.

6. Finesse the rickrack or ribbon so it lies flat and even as you come around the corner.

7. Repeat around the entire edge, stopping 2″ from where you started. Trim the rickrack or ribbon, leaving a 1″ overlap of the ends.

8. Fold under the raw end of the rickrack or ribbon ¼″ and secure with hot glue.

9. Hot glue the remaining section.

10. Turn the screen to the back and repeat the gluing.

11. For #12: Starting just past the clip, hot glue the leash to the center of the ribbon all the way around the screen.

12. For #12: Overlap the end of the leash with the clip and trim off any excess leash. Hot glue the clip on top of the end of the leash.

#13

pages 36-37

Lace With Butted Corners

1. Measure the sides of the screen, then add 2″ to this measurement.

2. Use the measurement from Step 1 to cut 2 pieces of lace.

3. Measure the top and bottom edges, then add 3″ to this measurement.

4. Use the measurement from Step 3 to cut 2 pieces of lace.

5. Working in short sections on the back of the screen, place a line of hot glue right next to the edge of the screen and align the bound edge of one of the short pieces of lace, right side up, with the side edge of the screen.

6. Trim the ends of the lace even with the edge of the screen. Repeat for the other short piece of lace.

7. Turn the screen to the front and repeat the gluing process from Step 5, adjusting the gathers.

8. With the long pieces, repeat Step 5 for the top and bottom edges of the screen.

9. Trim the ends of the lace, leaving a 1″ tail. Turn the screen to the front, fold the raw ends to the front, and hot glue.

10. Repeat the gluing process, adjusting the gathers.

Butted Corners

Nonskid Material
pages 38-39

Coated Kraft Paper
pages 44-45

1. Measure the sides of the screen, then add 2″ to this measurement.

2. For #15: Place 2 pieces of clear packing tape the length of the measurement from Step 1 on the kraft paper.

3. Use the measurement from Step 1 to cut 2 strips of tape-coated kraft paper or nonskid material 1½″ wide.

4. Measure the top and bottom edges, then add 2″ to this measurement.

5. For #15: Place 2 pieces of clear packing tape the length of the measurement from Step 4 on the kraft paper.

6. Use the measurement from Step 5 to cut 2 strips of tape-coated kraft paper or nonskid material 1½″ wide.

7. Fold the strips in half lengthwise.

8. Place a short strip over the side edge of the screen, lining up the fold on the strip with the edge of the screen. Trim the end of the strip even with the edge of the screen.

9. Hot glue the strip to the front side of the screen. Repeat for the other side strip.

10. Turn the screen to the back and repeat the gluing process.

11. Repeat for the top and bottom edges of the screen.

#16

Ribbon
pages 16-17

#17

Layered Trim/Ribbon
page 27

#18

Layered Ribbons
pages 42-43

Butted Corners

1. Measure the sides of the screen, then add 2″ to this measurement.

2. For #16: Use the measurement from Step 1 to cut 2 pieces of ribbon.

For #17: Use the measurement from Step 1 to cut 2 pieces of lace and 2 pieces of ribbon.

For #18: Use the measurement from Step 1 to cut 2 pieces of each width of ribbon.

3. Measure the top and bottom edges, then add 3″ to this measurement.

4. For #16: Use the measurement from Step 3 to cut 2 pieces of ribbon.

For #17: Use the measurement from Step 3 to cut 2 pieces of lace and 2 pieces of ribbon.

For #18: Use the measurement from Step 3 to cut 2 pieces of each width of ribbon.

5. For #17 and #18: Glue the wide ribbon to the lace or narrow ribbon.

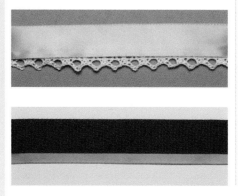

6. Repeat Step 5 for each remaining lace or ribbon pair.

7. Fold each piece of ribbon or layered ribbon in half lengthwise and press.

8. Place a short piece over the side edge of the screen, lining up the fold of the ribbon with the edge of the screen. Stitch or glue in place.

9. Trim the ends of the ribbon even with the edge of the screen. Repeat for the other short piece of ribbon.

10. Align the fold of a long piece of lace/ribbon with the top edge of the screen and glue in place. Trim the ends of the lace, leaving a 1″ tail.

11. Fold the tails to the back and stitch or glue. If gluing, repeat for the back of the screen.

12. Repeat for the bottom edge of the screen.

Prefolded Trim With Running Stitch on Wavy Edge and Rounded Corners

pages 34-35

#19

1. Measure around the screen, then add 12″ to this measurement.

2. Use the measurement from Step 1 to cut a piece of prefolded trim.

3. Place a pin in the center of a long edge of the trim.

4. Cut a piece of perle cotton thread twice as long as the cut trim.

5. Thread a needle with the perle cotton and insert the needle into the trim at the pin, next to the edge. Stitch through just one layer.

6. Pull half the length of the thread through the binding.

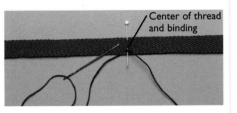

Center of thread and binding

7. Stitch a running stitch to one end of the binding. Remove the needle from the thread, leaving the thread tail.

8. Rethread the needle with the other end of the thread and rotate the binding 180°.

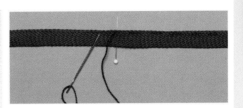

9. Stitch a running stitch to the other end of the binding. Remove the needle, leaving the thread tail.

10. Starting at the lower right corner, and working in short sections on the front of the screen, place a line of hot glue right next to the edge of the strip. Match the fold on the trim with the edge of the screen.

11. Pull the thread to help finesse the trim so it lies flat and even as you come around the corners.

12. Repeat around the entire edge, stopping 2″ from where you started.

13. Turn the screen to the back and glue the trim to the back of the screen. Trim, leaving ½″ extra.

14. Fold under the raw end of the trim ½″ and secure with hot glue. Be sure to catch the thread in the glue.

Turned-Under Edge With Square Corners

1. On the back of the screen, pull ½″ of the edge of the fabric away from the fusible all the way around the screen. Warm with an iron if necessary to soften the adhesive.

2. Starting on the top edge, fold the fabric from the front of the screen to the back of the screen and iron it to the fusible. Place a dab of hot glue to secure the corner. Repeat for all 4 sides.

3. Starting on the top edge, fold under the fabric from the back of the screen, so it comes just below the edge of the screen. Working in short sections, hot glue the fabric in place. Repeat for all 4 sides.

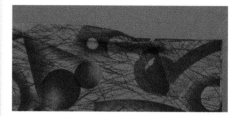

Special Techniques

Sleepytime Dolls Bed Pockets and Quilts

BED POCKETS

1. Cut 5 pieces of eyelet fabric $3\frac{1}{2}'' \times 5''$ for the sheets. With right sides together, fold each sheet in half to $3\frac{1}{2}'' \times 2\frac{1}{2}''$.

2. With the fold on the bottom edge, stitch the 2 side seams.

3. Turn right side out and press. Stitch the sheet to the wrong side of the eyelet trim.

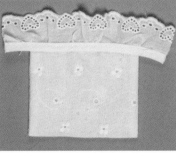

4. Fold the eyelet trim over the top edge of the sheet, wrap the raw ends to the back, and pin.

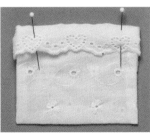

5. Position the sheet on the screen, with the bottom edge straight and the sides at an angle, forming a pocket. Hot glue in place. Add a hook-and-loop tape dot to secure the quilt to the pocket.

QUILTS

1. Cut 5 pieces of plaid fabric $4\frac{1}{2}'' \times 8\frac{1}{2}''$. Fold each piece in half with right sides together to $4\frac{1}{2}'' \times 4\frac{1}{4}''$.

2. Using a $\frac{1}{4}''$ seam allowance, stitch around the edge, leaving an opening for turning.

3. Turn right side out, turn under the seam allowance at the opening, and press.

4. Topstitch around the quilt next to the edge.

5. Tie, using perle cotton thread. Add a hook-and-loop tape dot to secure the quilt to the pocket.

2 Fast 4U Vehicle Pockets

1. Cut a piece of fabric 7″ × 42″ (if necessary, piece to this length) and fold in half lengthwise (3½″ × 42″).

2. Starting from the center, mark the strip as shown.

3. Fold on the pocket folding lines.

4. Stitch hook-and-loop dots to the front 1″ sections of the pockets.

5. Align the raw edges of the strip with the bottom and side edges of the screen and machine baste ⅛″ from the edges.

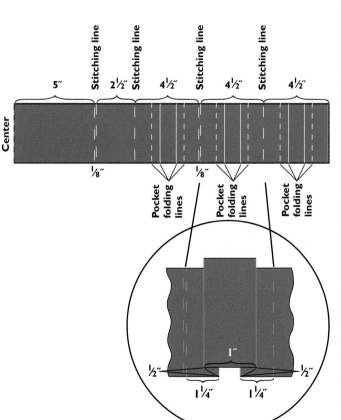

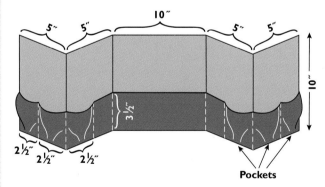

6. Stitch the hook-and-loop straps in position on the screen.

7. Stitch the pocket strip to the screen between the pockets and at the screen folds.

Resources

Materials and Supplies

Acme International Enterprises, Inc.
Mini-gadget small kitchen utensils
973-416-0400
www.acme-usa.com

All My Memories
Goodies buttons (fresh green, wisteria)
888-553-1998
www.allmymemories.com

American Traditional Designs
Small brass stencils
800-448-6656
www.americantraditional.com

Blumenthal Lansing Company
Favorite Findings buttons (white)
563-538-4211
www.buttonsplus.com

Creative Imagination self-adhesive letter dots
Poemstones by Sharon Soneff:
self-adhesive word and letter dots
800-942-6487
www.cigift.com

Darice
Foam rubber stars and letters, mirror tiles
800-321-1494
www.darice.com

Design Originals
Slide mounts
817-877-0067
www.d-originals.com

Dill Buttons
888-460-7555
www.dill-buttons.com

Dreamweaver Stencils and Lynell Harlow
Large brass stencils
909-824-8343
www.stencilwithstyle.com (retail)
www.dreamweaverstencils.com (wholesale)

Fibre-Craft Materials Corp.
Creative Hands sheet foam rubber
www.creativehands.net

Making Memories
Square buttons
801-294-0430
www.makingmemories.com

Poppy Fabric
Giant jumbo cotton rickrack
800-557-6779
www.poppyfabric.com

Renee's Garden
Flower seed packets
888-880-7228
www.reneesgarden.com

Scrapworks
Round and square spiral clips
801-363-1010
www.scrapworks.com

fast2fuse
Double-Sided Fusible
Stiff Interfacing
Available at your local quilt or craft store or from C&T Publishing.

Books

Photo Fun: Print Your Own Fabric for Quilts & Crafts, The Hewlett-Packard Company & Cyndy Lyle Rymer, C&T Publishing

More Photo Fun: Exciting New Ideas for Printing on Fabric for Quilts & Crafts, The Hewlett-Packard Company with Cyndy Lyle Rymer & Lynn Koolish, C&T Publishing

Fast, Fun & Easy Scrapbook Quilts, Sue Astroth, C&T Publishing

The Art of Fabric Books, Jan Bode Smiley, C&T Publishing

Quilting Supplies

Cotton Patch Mail Order
3405 Hall Lane, Dept. CTB
Lafayette, CA 94595
800-835-4418
925-283-7883
quiltusa@yahoo.com
www.quiltusa.com

Note: Fabrics shown may not be currently available since fabric manufacturers keep most fabrics in print for only a short time.

For more information, write for a free catalog:
C&T Publishing, Inc.
P.O. Box 1456
Lafayette, CA 94549
800-284-1114
ctinfo@ctpub.com
www.ctpub.com

About the Author

Liz Aneloski has been quilting since 1981 and crafting as long as she can remember. She loves combining techniques and materials to create unique and inspirational projects. She has been an editor at C&T Publishing since 1991 and lives in Northern California, where she grew up.

Other books by Liz Aneloski

Index